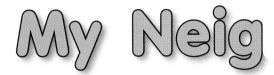

My Neig

by Frankie Hartley
illustrated by Lesley Breen Withrow

MW00789178

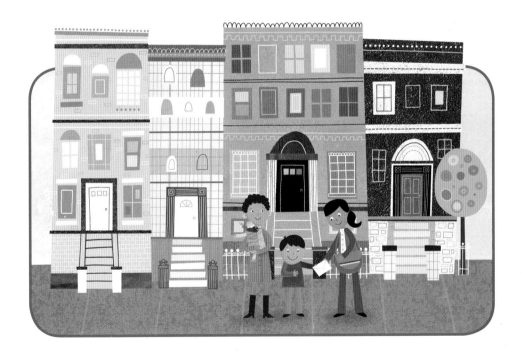

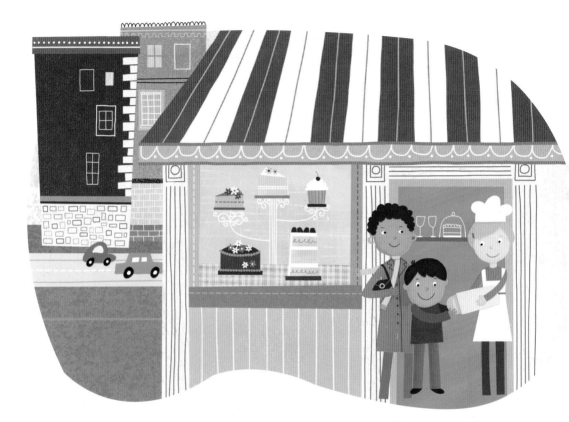

I do like .

bread

2

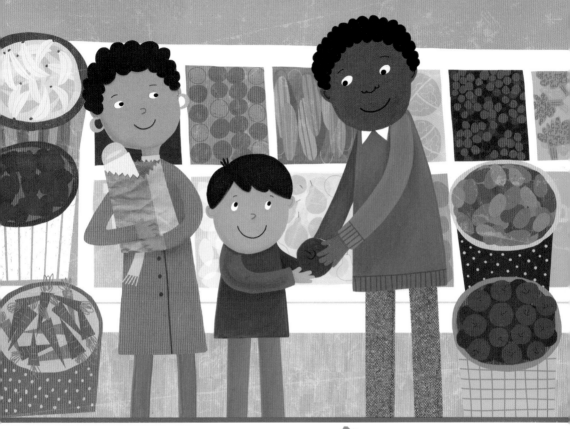

I do like .

apples

3

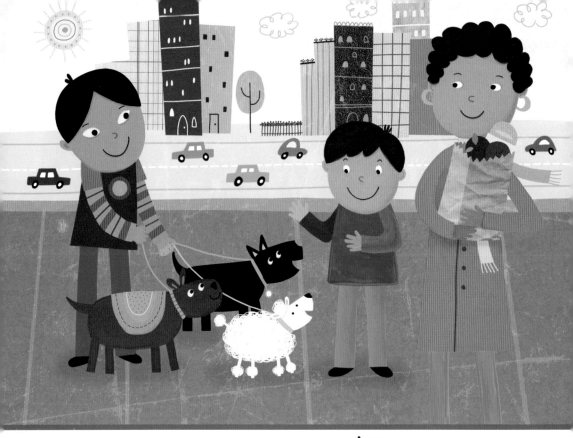

I do like .

dogs

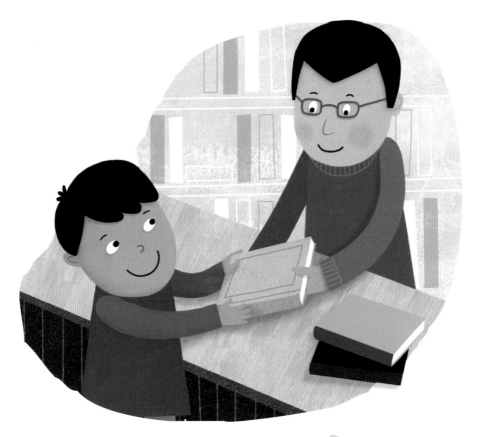

I do like .

books

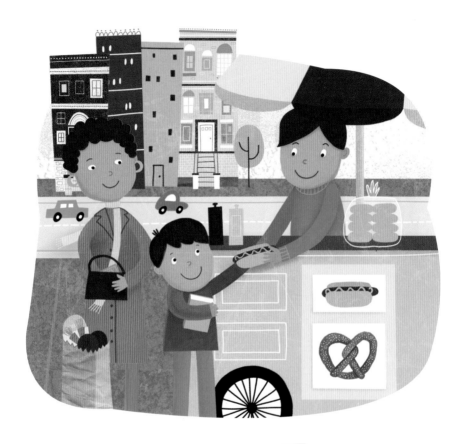

I do like 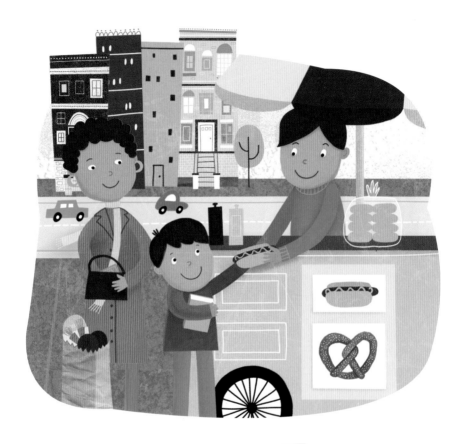.
hot dogs

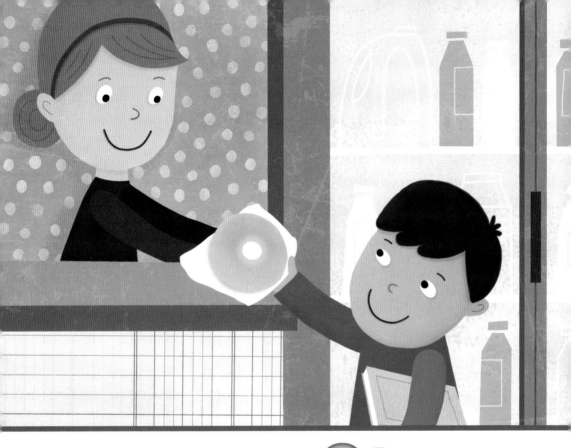

I do like 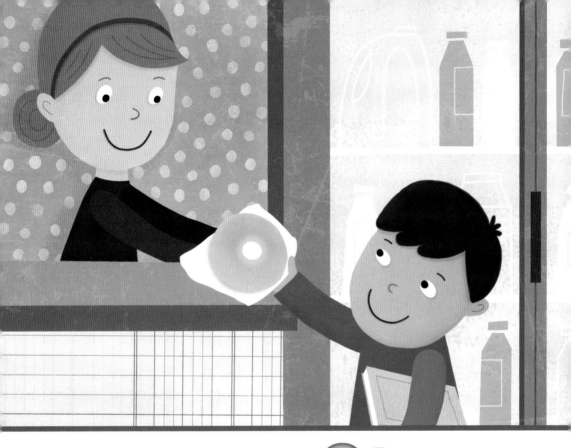 .
bagels

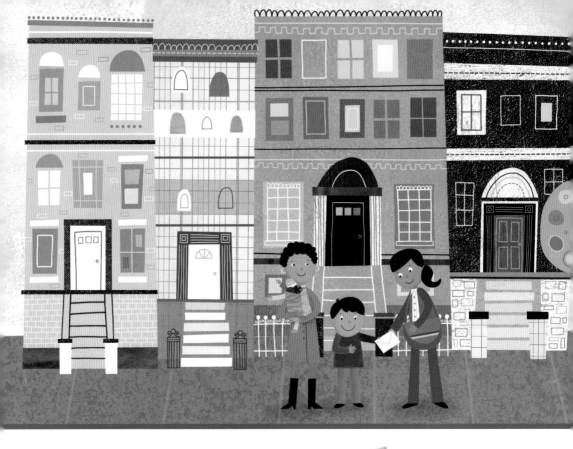

I do like .
letters